for

English

Boca Raton, Florida

DISCLAIMER:
This QuickStudy® Booklet is an outline only, and as such, cannot include every aspect of this subject. Use it as a supplement for course work and textbooks. BarCharts, Inc., its writers and editors are not responsible or liable for the use or misuse of the information contained in this booklet.

©2006 BarCharts, Inc.
ISBN 13: 9781423202592
ISBN 10: 1423202597

BarCharts® and QuickStudy® are registered trademarks of BarCharts, Inc.

Publisher:

BarCharts, Inc.
6000 Park of Commerce Boulevard, Suite D
Boca Raton, FL 33487
www.quickstudy.com

Printed in Thailand

Contents

Study Hints

NOTE TO STUDENT:
Use this QuickStudy® booklet to make the most of your studying time.

QuickStudy® examples offer detailed explanations; refer to them often to avoid problems.

Examples:
For the student <u>*the prepositional phrase*</u> *can be confusing* **in a sentence.**
- The prepositional phrase **for the student** modifies the <u>*subject phrase*</u>, and second prepositional phrase **in a sentence** modifies the verb.

QuickStudy® notes provide need-to-know information; read them carefully to better understand key concepts.

NOTES
If we were to take out the preposition then the sentence becomes: **She wondered what she would do next.** The noun clause thus becomes the object of the verb **wondered** and the sentence takes on a more urgent form.

Take your learning to the next level with QuickStudy®!

Subjects

Nouns

■ Proper Nouns

Name a specific person, place or object. They begin with an uppercase letter.

- ◆ **John**
- ◆ **Mercury**
- ◆ **California**

■ Common Nouns

Name a nonspecific person, place, or object; they do not begin with an uppercase letter.

- ◆ **boy**
- ◆ **planet**
- ◆ **state**

Pronouns

Take the position and function of nouns, but do not specifically name.

- ◆ *He* fed the cat.
- ◆ *She* fed the cat.
- ◆ *It* got extremely fat.
- ◆ *They* wish they had fed it less.

Nominative Elements
■ **Verbals**
  ◆ **Gerunds** (-ing form of the verb)
    • ***Reading*** travel books is my hobby.
    • ***Traveling*** by train is part of my daily routine.
  ◆ **Infinitives** (to, plus the verb)
    • ***To read a travel book*** brings me pleasure.
    • ***To travel by train*** can be fun.
■ **Noun Clauses**
  That one needs a clear goal is stressed in college preparatory classes.

General Rules
■ All inflected forms must be in subjective case.
■ Gender is important with subject pronouns.
  ◆ ***John*** is proud of the school ***he*** attended.
■ Number is important for agreement of subject and verb.
  ◆ The ***woman was*** tall.
  ◆ The ***women were*** tall.
  ◆ The ***man and the woman were*** tall.

Specific Rules
■ Some pronouns always take singular verbs.
  ◆ ***each, someone, either, neither, somebody, nobody, everybody, anyone, nothing***
■ Some pronouns always take plural verbs.
  ◆ ***both, few, several, many***
■ **Collective nouns** thought of as a *single unit* require a *singular verb*. **Collective nouns** with *identified parts* require a *plural verb*.
  ◆ The ***group is*** going to the show.
  ◆ The ***men are*** going to the show.

■ Generally, *subjects* appear before the verb and may be separated by *modifiers* or prepositional phrases. To determine a subject, answer *who* or *what* about the construction being analyzed.

◆ *John* walks.

◆ *The train* runs.

◆ *John*, who is late for the train, runs.

Verbs (Predicates)

> **NOTES**
> **Verb:** what a subject is doing; what is being done to it; a state of being

The 5 Properties of Verbs

■ Person
A **verb** is in the **same <u>person</u>** as its subject.
- ◆ <u>First</u> person: *I am hoping for rain.*
- ◆ <u>Second</u> person: *You are hoping for rain.*
- ◆ <u>Third</u> person: *He is hoping for rain.*

■ Number
- ◆ A **singular verb** requires a singular subject.
  A **plural verb** requires a plural subject.
  - When two singular subjects are joined by *and,* the verb is plural. **Exception:** when two singular subjects are connected by and present a single idea, the verb may be singular.
  - When two singular subjects are connected by *or, either...or,* or *neither...nor,* the verb is singular.
  - When two plural subjects are connected by *or, either...or,* or *neither...nor,* the verb is plural.
  - The verb agrees with the *nearer subject* of a compound sentence which has both a singular and a plural word joined by *or* or *nor.*

- When the **subject** and the <u>subjective complement</u> (predicate adjectives, predicate nominatives that follow linking verbs and refer to the subject) are different in number, the verb agrees with the **subject**.

  > *The **books** that I received **were** <u>the most appreciated.</u>*

◆ *Every* or *many* before a word or series of words is followed by a singular verb.

  - *Every man, woman, and child **was** asked to donate.*

◆ When the <u>subject</u> comes after the verb, as in sentences beginning with **here is, there is,** and **where is,** make sure that the verb agrees with the subject.

  - *There **are** three <u>**courses**</u> of action we can take.*

■ **Voice**

◆ **Active Voice:** <u>Subject</u> is **acting**.
  - <u>*Lightning*</u> *struck the barn.*

◆ **Passive Voice:** <u>Subject</u> is **acted upon**.
  - *The <u>barn</u> **was struck** by lightning.*
  - The *passive form* always consists of some form of the verb *be* plus the past participle.

■ **Mood**

◆ **Indicative:** makes a statement or asks a question.
  - *It is forty miles to Gainesville, but we'll get there in time.*

◆ **Imperative:** expresses a command, request, suggestion, entreaty, etc. where subject (usually the pronoun **you**) is understood.
  - *Stop! Please sign the form before returning it.*

◆ **Subjunctive:** equals the past tense in structure and is used after *if* and *wish* when the statement is contrary to reality.
  • *I wish I <u>**were**</u> a rich woman.*
  • *If I <u>**knew**</u> her number, I <u>**would**</u> call her.*

■ **Tense**
  ◆ Made from the principal parts of verbs
  ◆ Three forms are:
    • **Present tense or present infinitive:** *do, give, ring, throw*
    • **Past tense:** *did, gave, rang, threw*
    • **Past participle:** *done, given, rung, thrown*

Classes & Types of Verbs

■ A **transitive verb** takes an <u>object.</u>
  ◆ ***Push*** *this <u>button</u> if you **want** a <u>light</u>.*

■ An **<u>intransitive</u> verb** does not take an object.
  ◆ *The sun **shone** brightly.*

■ A verb can be transitive or intransitive in different sentences.

■ An **<u>auxiliary</u> verb** is used before main verbs to form the passive voice, produce certain tenses, ask questions, make negative statements, and express shades of meaning.
  ◆ *They <u>have been</u> **studying** diligently.*
  ◆ *I <u>**do**</u> not **like** the course.*
  ◆ A **<u>phrasal verb</u>** is more than one word long and combines one or more **auxiliary** verbs with a main verb.
    • *They <u>**were given**</u> many opportunities.*

■ **Linking or inactive verbs** link the subject with a predicate noun, predicate pronoun, or a <u>predicate adjective</u> and are always **intransitive:** *He **looked** <u>sad.</u>*

◆ A **linking verb** states that one thing is equal to another and thus requires that the ***<u>subjective case</u>*** be used: *This **is** <u>he.</u>*

Modifiers

NOTES
Modifier: definitive element used to modify other words

Adjectives & Adjectival Elements
Used to Modify Nouns or Pronouns

■ **Prepositional phrases, verbal phrases, and adjective dependent clauses** change the image made by the noun or nominative element by itself.

■ **Proper adjectives** are formed from a **proper** noun.
  ◆ *French, Democrat, etc.*

■ **Demonstrative adjectives** answer the question **which one**?
  ◆ *this, that, these, those* (also called pronouns)

■ **Descriptive adjectives** answer the question **what kind**?
  ◆ *big, small, red, etc.*

■ **Quantitative adjectives** answer the question **how many**?
  ◆ *one, three, some, few, several* (also called pronouns)

■ **Qualitative adjectives** answer the question **how much**?
 ◆ *little, much, considerable*

■ In comparing the quality of nouns, adjective **change by degrees**.
 ◆ The **positive degree** covers one item: *big, good*
 ◆ **Comparative degree** covers two items: *bigger, better*
 ◆ **Superlative degree** covers three or more: *biggest, best*

■ A **predicate adjective** follows any **linking** or **state of being** verb: *The men **were sick** from eating the raw oysters.*

Adverbs & Adverbial Elements
Used to Modify Verbs, Adjectives or Other Adverbs

■ **Prepositional phrases, verbal phrases, or adverbial dependent clauses** add descriptive elements to a sentence.

■ **Adverbs** answer one or more of these questions:
 ◆ How? (by what **manner**?) *quickly, slowly, fast*
 ◆ When? (at what **time**?) *now, then, never*
 ◆ Where? (at what **location**?) *here, there, down, up*
 ◆ To what extent does a thing have some **quality**?
 ◆ To what extent does the adverb express **quantity**?

■ Adverbs **follow** the **verb**.
  ◆ *John walked **slowly.***
  ◆ *John walked **faster than Peter.***

■ Adverbs modifying adjectives and adverbs **precede** the word being modified.
  ◆ *John walked **surprisingly** slowly for someone so tall.*

■ One syllable adverbs are compared by adding **-er** or **-est.**
  ◆ *John walked **slower** than I did.*
  ◆ *John walked **slowest** of all.*

■ Adverbs of two or more syllables add **more** or **most.**
  ◆ *John walks **more slowly** than I.*
  ◆ *I am **most happy** to know that.*

4

Objects

NOTES

Object: completing element in a sentence

■ **Direct Objects**

Noun, pronoun, or nominative element that receives the action expressed in the verb.

◆ *I have read the **book**.*

■ **Indirect Objects** Noun, pronoun, or nominative element **for** or **to whom** or **to what** the action in the verb was done.

◆ *I read the **class** the entire book.*

■ **Objects of Prepositions**

Answer the question **whom** or **what** *after* the <u>preposition.</u>

◆ *John traveled <u>to</u> **the country in his car**.*

■ **Objects of Verbals**

(Gerunds, Participles, Infinitives)

Are nouns, pronouns, or nominative elements.

◆ *Knowing nothing about making noodles, **I bought some**.*

■ **Pronouns as Objects**

◆ All personal pronouns used as objects must be in the **objective case:** *The call for **him** and **me** came at noon.*

◆ **Who** is the **subject** form: *Who sent the fax?* **Whom** is the **object** form: *To whom should I send the fax?*

13

5 Words

■ Background

- ◆ Words are composed of sounds **(phonemes)** to which meaning is attached.
- ◆ The range of human sounds is codified in the International Phonetic Alphabet.
  - • Some symbols are similar to the alphabet; some appear to be strange squiggles.
  - • One can learn the symbols and approximate a given sound, but variances in stress and pause will not yield a fluent rendering of a language.
- ◆ Sounds in predictable patterns become words. Meaning is attached by users and listeners of a particular language.

■ Suffix & Prefix

- ◆ Combinations of sounds which appear at the beginning and/or end of words to alter meanings, indicate functions, and to signal particular use in a construction.
- ◆ Suffixes **-s** or **-es** are plural when attached to a noun and singular when attached to a verb.
- ◆ **-ly** signals an adverb or modifier

- ◆ **-er** signals comparative degree of adjective
- ◆ **-est** signals superlative degree of adjective
- ◆ **-ed** frequently signals past tense of a verb

■ Marker Words (Articles)

- ◆ **A, an,** or **the** are noun markers that precede the noun.
- ◆ Auxiliary verbs **can, may, be, do,** plus a verb, will always mark a verb.
- ◆ Subordinate conjunctions **after, although, as, because, if,** mark a dependent clause.

Phrases

6

■ Prepositional Phrases
- ◆ Made up of a preposition plus its object and any modifiers.
- ◆ Used as modifiers (adjectives or adverbs).

■ Common Prepositions

about	before	except	off	under
above	behind	for	on	until
according to	below	from	out	up
across	beneath	in	outside	upon
after	beside	in place of	over	with
against	between	inside	past	within
along	beyond	into	since	without
among	by	like	through	
around	down	near	to	
at	during	of	toward	

Examples:
For the student <u>the prepositional phrase</u> can be confusing **in a sentence.**

- • The prepositional phrase **for the student** modifies the <u>subject phrase</u>, and second prepositional phrase **in a sentence** modifies the verb.

■ Verbal Phrases

- ◆ Verb forms not used as verbs.
- ◆ Because they are verb forms, verbals retain many of the properties of verbs by taking objects, by having their own subjects and by being modified by adverbs.

■ Infinitive Phrases

- ◆ Infinitive (**to + verb**), which can be used as a noun, an adjective, or an adverb.
- ◆ *To read these papers will take a long time.*
  - • The infinitive *to read* is the subject of the sentence.
- ◆ *She <u>wanted</u> to read the book.*
  - • The infinitive *to read* is the direct object of the <u>verb</u>.
- ◆ *She had money to spend.*
  - • The infinitive *to spend* modifies *money.*
- ◆ *I am ready to write the paper now.*
  - • The infinitive *to write* modifies the adjective *ready.*
- ◆ The infinitive may have its own subject and object.
- ◆ The infinitive **to be** has special rules.
  - • The subject of an infinitive is in the objective case.
  - • Because the linking verb requires the same case both before and after it, the noun or pronoun used as a complement must be in the objective case.

■ Gerund Phrases

◆ The gerund (**-ing** form of the verb) is used as a noun.

◆ *Walking is a healthy exercise.*

   • The gerund **walking** is the subject of the verb **is**.

◆ *Proper shoes are needed* **for** *comfortable* **walking**.

   • The gerund **walking** is the object of the preposition **for**.

■ Participial Phrases

◆ The participle (**present, past,** or **perfect participle** of the **verb**) is used as an adjective.

◆ *The* **girl talking** *on the phone is Mary*.

   • The participle **talking** modifies **girl**.

◆ *The* **letter signed** *by John was ready for the mail.*

   • The participle **signed** modifies the noun **letter**.

◆ *The report,* **accurately written,** *was approved by him*.

   • The participle **written**, plus **accurately**, describes report.

Clauses

7

NOTES
Clause: group of related words that contains a subject and a verb

■ Independent Clauses
- ◆ Meet the above qualifications for clauses.
- ◆ May be regarded as sentences since they make sense.
  - • ***She had not finished the paper*** and was sure to get a low grade.

■ Dependent Clauses
- ◆ Meet the above qualifications for clauses.
- ◆ Do not make sense and are regarded as fragments also called **subordinate** clauses.
  - • *Because she had not finished the paper.*

Types of Dependent Clauses
■ Noun Clauses
Noun clauses are dependent clauses used like nouns:
- ◆ ***That she had not finished the paper*** *was the reason for her low grade.* (The noun clause ***that she had not finished the paper*** is used as the subject of the sentence.)

◆ *I know **what I will do today.*** (The noun clause ***what I will do today*** is used as the direct object of the verb *know*.)

◆ *She wondered about **what she should do next.*** (The noun clause ***what she should do next*** is the object of the preposition *about*.)

Examples:
If we were to take out the preposition then the sentence becomes: ***She wondered what she would do next***. The noun clause thus becomes the object of the verb **wondered** and the sentence takes on a more urgent form.

■ **Adjective Clauses**
Adjective clauses are used to point out or describe any noun or pronoun in the sentence.

◆ A relative pronoun (***who, whom, whose, which, that***) always introduces an adjective clause.

◆ Adjective clauses may be **restrictive** or **nonrestrictive.**

◆ *The car **that is parked by the curb** belongs to me.* (The adjective clause, ***that is parked by the curb,*** modifies *car* in a restrictive way.)

◆ *The car, **that is parked by the curb,** belongs to me.* (Setting off the adjective clause with **commas [,]** is nonrestrictive and subtly changes the meaning of the sentence since, in the first sentence we are saying that **only the car that is parked by the curb belongs to me.** In the second sentence we are saying that **the car belongs to me, and, by the way, it is parked at the curb**.)

■ Adverb Clauses

Adverb clauses are used as adverbs.

◆ **Adverb clauses** are introduced by subordinate conjunctions *(after, although, as, as if, because, before, if, since, so that, that, unless, until, when, where, while).*

◆ When the adverb clause begins a sentence, it is set off by a comma.

◆ *Because he was late, she was angry.* (The adverbial clause *because he was late* modifies the adjective *angry.*)

◆ *She was angry because he was late.* (This expresses the same idea without requiring the comma, since the subordinate conjunction does not come at the beginning of the sentence.)

Connectors

8

NOTES

Connector: joining element in a sentence

■ **Conjunctions**

Joining words that link parts of sentences

◆ **Coordinating conjunctions** join like parts of words, phrases, and clauses.

• *Joe **and** Mary went to the show.*
• *You will find it in the cupboard **or** under the counter.*
• *Jim shut the door, **but** he did not lock it.*

◆ **Correlative conjunctions** join like parts and come in **pairs.**

• ***Not** Tom **but** his brother won the tournament.*
• ***Neither** Mary **nor** Jane were impressed by this.*

◆ **Subordinate conjunctions** are used to introduce **adverb clauses** and link them to the main clause.

• *Not only Tom but his brother won the tournament, **because** they practiced hard.*

■ Conjunctive Adverbs

Used to join main clauses

◆ Conjunctive adverbs are **always preceded by a semicolon [;]** and are always **followed by a comma [,].**

Examples:

Accordingly, consequently, furthermore, however, nevertheless, etc.

- *She knew her lack of studying would be a detriment; **nevertheless**, she took the test.*
- *She was sick and tired of all this nagging about studying; **however,** she did find this guide useful.*

Sentences

NOTES

Sentence: group of related words that has a subject (present or understood) and a verb, and that expresses a complete thought

Kinds of Sentences

■ **Declarative Sentence**
- ◆ Makes a <u>statement</u>.
- ◆ *Today is the day before the long holiday.*

■ **Imperative Sentence**
- ◆ Gives a <u>command</u>.
- ◆ *Please close the door on your way out.*

■ **Interrogative Sentence**
- ◆ Asks a <u>question</u>.
- ◆ *Who was that woman?*

■ **Exclamatory Sentence**
- ◆ Expresses <u>strong feeling</u>.
- ◆ Ends with an exclamation point.
- ◆ *What a beautiful morning!*

Sentence Patterns

■ **Pattern 1 (S + V) [subject] + [verb]**
  - ◆ The subject may be compound.
  - ◆ The verb may be compound.
  - ◆ ***John ran.*** (*John* is the subject and *ran* is the verb).
  - ◆ ***John** and **Peter ran** and **fell down.***

■ **Pattern 2 (S + V + D.O.)**
  [subject + verb + direct object]
  - ◆ Any of the elements may be compound.
  - ◆ The verb represents direct or indirect action, active or passive voice.
  - ◆ ***John ran the race.*** (*John* is the subject, *ran* is the verb, and *race* is the direct object)
  - ◆ *The **race** was **run** by **John**.*

■ **Pattern 3 (S + V + I.O. + D.O.)**
  [subject + verb + indirect object + direct object]
  - ◆ Any of the elements may be compound.
  - ◆ ***Dad paid the clerk the sales tax.*** (*Dad* is the subject, *paid* is the verb, *clerk* is the indirect object and *sales tax* is the direct object.)

■ **Pattern 4 (S + V + S.C.)**
  [subject + verb + subjective complement]
  - ◆ Any of the elements may be compound.
  - ◆ The verb must be linking - have no action.
  - ◆ ***Jane is my attorney.*** (*Jane* is the subject, *is* [linking verb] is the verb, and *attorney* is a predicate nominative.)
  - ◆ ***The water is blue.*** (*Water* is the subject, *is* [linking verb] is the verb, and *blue* is a predicate adjective.)

Sentence Forms

■ **Simple Sentence (an independent clause)**
Contains a subject and a verb and expresses <u>only one complete thought</u>.
Either the subject or the verb may be compound.
◆ *John slept.*
◆ *John and Bobbie slept.*

■ **Compound Sentence**
Contains <u>two or more</u> independent clauses and can express more than one complete thought.
◆ Compound sentences are **joined by coordinating conjunctions** (*and, or, nor, for, so, yet, but*) or a **semicolon [;]** when no coordinating conjunction is present.
  • *Bobbie likes watching TV, but she prefers going to the movies.*
  • *Bobbie likes watching TV, she enjoys exercising on the treadmill, and she adores the smell of puppy breath.*

NOTES
Using **only** a comma[,] between the two or more independent clauses of a compound sentence will result in a **comma splice error**.
Error - Bobbie likes John, she loves vacations.

◆ Placing no punctuation between independent clauses which do not have a coordinating conjunction will result in an error called **"run-on"** or **"fused."**
Error - Bobbie likes movies John likes vacations.

■ **Complex Sentence**
Contains an independent and a <u>dependent clause.</u>
- ◆ **Adverb clauses** appearing at the beginning of a complex sentence are set off by a comma. *<u>If you are going to walk</u>, be sure to stay on the path.*

■ **Compound/Complex Sentence**
Contains at least two independent clauses and at least one dependent clause.
- ◆ *If you are going to walk, be sure to stay on the path; you won't get lost.*

Commas

> **NOTES**
> **Comma:** punctuation mark that separates and encloses phrases and clauses

With Coordinate Conjunctions
and, but, or, nor, for, so, yet

■ Separate Main Clauses within a Sentence
- ◆ Mary counsels students, **and** she volunteers at the local hospital.
- ◆ John planned to invest his tax return, **but** he bought a computer instead.
- ◆ Doug will play the game, **or** he will mow the lawn.
- ◆ I don't smoke, **nor** do I eat near people who smoke.
- ◆ Sandra won't be going with us, **for** she returned her application too late.
- ◆ The bank lowered its interest rates, **so** we decided to refinance our mortgage.
- ◆ I haven't seen the new house, **yet** I know how to get there.

■ **Do Not Use Commas before Conjunctions That Link Phrases Other than Complete Sentences**

◆ Mary counsels students **and** delivers meals to shut-ins.

◆ Two inches of snow **and** a glazing of ice covered the streets.

With Introductory Elements

■ **Commas Separate Elements That Introduce and Modify Sentences**

◆ **After looking at several cars,** Michael decided on a sporty model.

■ **Commas Can Be Omitted after Short Introductory Elements If There Is No Risk of Misreading**

◆ **After I moved** I lost contact with my high school pals.

With Other Elements

■ **Dates**

◆ On **December 7, 1941,** Japanese war planes bombed Pearl Harbor.

◆ On **7 December 1941,** Japanese warplanes bombed Pearl Harbor. *(Notice that military dating does not require commas.)*

◆ On **Wednesday, December 28, 1994,** I will celebrate my 30th birthday.

■ **Addresses & Place Names**

◆ The President of the United States lives at **1600 Pennsylvania Ave., Washington, D.C.**

■ **Numbers**
- The city marina cost **$8,479,000** to construct.
- Jill's dress has over **2,500** hand-sewn beads.
- Martin planted 1500 marigold plants.

  (With four-digit numbers, commas are optional.)

■ **Quotations**

Commas ordinarily separate a quotation from its source, such as *he said* or *she said.*
- John F. Kennedy said, **"Ask not what your country can do for you; ask what you can do for your country."**
- **"Sometimes love is stronger than a man's convictions,"** wrote Isaac Bashevis Singer.
- "I never forget a face," **said Groucho Marx,** "but in your case I'll make an exception."

■ **Parenthetical Expressions**

John's new car, **in my opinion**, is a lemon.

■ **Nouns of Direct Address**
- **Adam**, do you want to plant the palms this afternoon?

■ **Do Not Use a Comma with Identifying Words That Interrupt Main Clauses in a Quotation**
- "Don't speak to me," she sighed. "Your words are meaningless."

With Adjectives

■ **Coordinate Adjectives Modify Nouns Separately**

◆ We felt the **salty, humid** air near the beach.

◆ Martha created a **three-tiered, white, flower-covered** wedding cake for Jason and Renee. *(Coordinate adjectives can be joined with and (salty and humid; three-tiered and white and flower covered, and their positions can be changed without altering the meaning of the sentence.)*

■ **Cumulative Adjectives Do Not Require a Comma**

◆ Adam bought **two tall** palms.

◆ I found a shard from an **ancient Greek** urn.

◆ Marissa planned an **amazingly detailed, truly exotic** Halloween costume. *(There are two sets of cumulative adjectives in this sentence that function separately to modify "costume.")*

■ **Adding Commas to a String of Cumulative Adjectives or Changing Their Order Results in an Awkward Construction**

◆ Adam bought **two, tall** palms.

◆ Adam bought **tall, two** palms.

With Nonrestrictive Phrases & Appositives

■ **Nonrestrictive Elements Can Be Omitted without Changing Meaning**

◆ Frank's new aquarium, **a marine tank,** hosts brilliant coral and brightly colored fish.

◆ **Awakened by a strange noise,** Alan wondered if he remembered to lock the door when he went to bed. *("Marine tank" and "Awakened by a strange noise" are not absolutely necessary to the meaning of the sentences.)*

■ **Do Not Use Commas to Set Off Restrictive Elements**
   ◆ The first house **on the left** is for sale. *(The phrase "on the left" is essential to the meaning of the sentence.)*
   ◆ Those people **who have already purchased** tickets may enter the theater now. *("Who have already purchased tickets" is essential to the meaning of the sentence.)*

With Parallel Words, Phrases & Appositives

■ The department store offered **a suit, a shirt, and a tie** for one low price.

■ The kitten stalked the ball of yarn **behind the curtain, over the television, and under the table.**

■ Marie offered her students a treat **if they would complete their assignment, if they would clean their desks, and if they would stack their books neatly.**

Comma Misuses
Misreadings & Omissions

■ **Use Commas to Prevent Misreadings and to Clarify Meaning in a Sentence**

◆ **To Susan,** Jason's choice of costume was unacceptable.

◆ **As soon as we left,** Marilyn closed the store.

■ **Commas Can Indicate an Omission:**

◆ Helen bought a new television; Mark, **a** laser printer; and Sarah, **a** stereo system.

Unnecessary Commas

◆ **Unnecessary Commas Can Be As Confusing as Leaving Out Required Commas.** *(For instance, if you separate a subject and verb or an adjective and the word it modifies with a comma, your reader will have to spend time figuring out which ideas go together.)*

     NOT   *Billy and Marcia, built a log home.*

     BUT   *Billy and Marcia built a log home.*

◆ *Do Not Place a Comma Before a Coordinating Conjunction and a Phrase [see "With Coordinate Conjunctions"].*

     NOT   *After school Samuel likes to finish his homework, and watch TV for a few hours.*

     BUT   *After school Samuel likes to finish his homework and watch TV for a few hours.*

     OR   *After school Samuel likes to finish his homework, and then he spends a few hours watching TV.*

NOTES
Notice that in the first example, the comma separates a compound verb, rather than two independent clauses.

Semicolons

11

Connect Main Clauses

◼ **Join Related Main Clauses When a Coordinating Conjunction Is Not Used.**

◆ I will not paint the house; **you can't make me.**

◆ Sally built a tree house; **she painted it blue.** *(Main clauses joined with a comma constitute a comma splice. Use a semicolon or separate the clauses into two complete sentences.)*

◼ **Work with Conjunctive Adverbs to Join Main Clauses**

◆ I would like to go to the museum with you; **however,** I must visit my dentist instead.

◆ Jim had given much thought to his future; **therefore,** it came as no surprise when he returned to school.

◆ The audience was sparse; **in fact,** there were only five people.

◆ I want to travel this summer; **accordingly,** I will have to save money this winter.

◆ Six people saw the bandit leaving the store; **moreover,** one customer even got his tag number.

37

■ Separate Items in Series That Contain Commas
- ◆ I packed my suitcase with **old, comfortable jeans; rugged, warm sweaters; and new, freshly starched shirts.**

■ Do Not Use Semicolons to Separate Unparallel Items

NOT   *Before starting the engine; Bill cleaned the windshield.*

BUT   *Before starting the engine,* **Bill cleaned the windshield.**

This sentence is made up of a *dependent clause* and an **independent clause;** therefore, the sentence does not require a semicolon to separate the clauses. One comma will do.

■ Separate Coordinate Clauses When They Are Joined by Transitional Words and Phrases

accordingly	afterwards	again
besides	consequently	doubtless
eventually	evidently	furthermore
however	moreover	nevertheless
otherwise	perhaps	therefore
for example	for instance	in addition

Colons

NOTES
Colons: end main clauses and/or introduce additions and modifications

Specific Uses

Examples:
- ◆ Frank introduced four kinds of fish into his new aquarium: three angels, six tetras, a pair of Bala sharks, and a spotted catfish.
- ◆ After a few months, Frank encountered a problem with his new aquarium set-up: algae growth.
- ◆ Tamara suggested a solution: "I keep quite a few snails in my aquarium. They eat the excess algae."

■ **Do Not Function Inside a Main Clause**

    NOT Frank's favorite fish is: the angel fish.
    BUT Frank's favorite fish is the angel fish.

■ **Link Independent Clauses When the Second Modifies the First**
Frank learned a serious lesson about aquarium maintenance: do not overfeed fish as this causes the water to cloud.

(The reader wants an explanation of the "serious lesson," which is provided in the second clause.)

■ **Other Uses**
   ◆ Business letter salutation - **Dear Mr. Brown:**
   ◆ Title and subtitle - **Dudes: My Story**
   ◆ Biblical citation - **Genesis 1:1**
   ◆ Bibliographic entries - **Boston: Houghton Mifflin Co.**

13 Apostrophes

NOTES
Apostrophe: punctuation mark used to show possession

Main Uses

■ **Add " 's " to form the possessive of singular and plural nouns and indefinite pronouns that do not end in s or with an s or a z sound.**

◆ My **mother's** purse held many treasures. *(the purse owned by my mother)*

◆ Can anyone's dog enter the Kennel show? (*dog is owned by anyone*)

◆ **The Women's League** is very active. *(The possessive form of women, a plural, takes an 's.)*

■ **Add " 's " to form the possessive of singular nouns ending in s or with an s or z sound.**

◆ We listened to the stereo in **Chris's** new car.

◆ **Liz's** dress was the sensation of the party. **(add only an apostrophe if the extra [s] creates an awkward pronunciation)**

Examples:
◆ *The Bible speaks admiringly of **Moses'** wisdom.*
◆ ***Jesus'** compassion was boundless.*
◆ Possessive forms of Moses and Jesus use the apostrophe, only: **Moses'/Jesus'**

■ **Add only an apostrophe to form the possessive of plural nouns ending in [s] or with an *s* or *z* sound.**
  ◆ The **cats'** toys were spread around the room.
  ◆ The latest car designs were engineered for **drivers'** comfort.

■ **To form the possessive of compound nouns, add ['s] to only the last word.**
  ◆ My **mother-in-law's** furniture was imported from Havana.
  ◆ Webster's **brother-in-law's** office was vandalized.

■ **Make only the last noun possessive to show joint possession.**
  ◆ **James and Susan's** dog chased our cat. *(The dog belongs to both James and Susan.)*

■ **Make both nouns possessive to show individual ownership.**
  ◆ **James's** and **Susan's** cars were both vandalized.

Other Uses

■ **Do not use an apostrophe with possessive pronouns.**
  ◆ **Ours** is the bright red mustang. (Not "Our's")

■ **Use an apostrophe to form the plural of letters, numbers, and abbreviations.**
  ◆ Phillip's **t's** look like his **i's**.
  ◆ We heard **bravo's** throughout the arena.

■ **Use an apostrophe to indicate contractions.**
  ◆ **I'm ok'd** to enter the restricted zone.
  ◆ The **'92** hurricane left a wide swath of damage through the Miami area.
  ◆ Strangely enough, we never had the opportunity to try **fish 'n' chips** while we were in London.

14 Quotation Marks

> **NOTES**
> **Quotation Marks:** punctuation marks used to set off quotations and titles

Direct & Indirect

■ **Enclose a Direct Quotation**

◆ Martha whispered quietly, **"I'm scared of the dark."**

◆ **"When,"** she breathed, **"do we get out of here?"**

◆ **"What if we get stuck in this place?"** she asked.

◆ **"I knew I should have taken up spelunking."**

■ **Capitalize the First Word of a Direct Quotation**

■ **Do Not Capitalize the First Word** in the second part of an interrupted quotation *unless* the second part begins a new sentence.

■ **Indirect Quotations Do Not Require Quotation Marks**

◆ **Father said that we should be frugal with our money.**

Enclose Other Forms of Quoted Material

■ **Article, Essay Titles and Short Stories**
   ◆ The current edition of *Vanity Fair* contains an article entitled **"Raider of the Lost Art."** *(Do not put quotation marks around titles of your own compositions.)*

■ **Chapter Titles**
   ◆ Susan quoted from chapter three of Carole Jackson's *Color Me Beautiful,* **"The Seasonal Palettes."**

■ **Song Titles**
   ◆ The Commodores' **"Three Times a Lady"** was the number one hit when I graduated from high school.

■ **Most Poem Titles**
   ◆ T.S. Eliot's **"The Love Song of J. Alfred Prufrock"** remains a landmark poem of the 20th century. (Longer poems, such as Eliot's <u>Waste Land,</u> are underlined or italicized.)

■ **Television and Radio Episode Titles**
   ◆ More people saw **"Going Home,"** the final episode of *M.A.S.H.*, than any other television show to date.

■ **Special Phrases, Words or Sentences**
   ◆ The phrase **"rule of thumb"** has a violent history.
   ◆ Marci pronounced **"accept"** as **"except."**
   ◆ The infamous declaration **"Let them eat cake"** represents the arrogance of the French Aristocracy.

Indented Quotes

■ **Direct quotations longer than four typed lines** are set off as block quotations by indenting ten spaces from the left margin and double spacing.

Examples:

There are many reasons why a pond ecosystem fails. For instance, industrial pollution might disrupt the "natural bio-diversity of the system." Another problem, due in part to industrial pollution, is acid rain, which acidifies the pond system.

(Indented passages do not require quotation marks unless they appear within the text.)

With Other Punctuation

■ **The period and comma** are always placed inside the ending quotation marks.

◆ He said, "Let's go to the beach today."

■ **The question mark and exclamation point** are placed within the quotation marks only when they refer to the quoted material.

◆ Frank asked, "When can I add fish to the tank?"

15

End Punctuation

Full sentences require end punctuation marks.*

■ **Periods End Most Sentences in English**
 ◆ Mary asked us about selling her house.

■ **Polite requests that do not require a "yes" or "no" answer should use a period**
 ◆ Would you please clean your room.

■ **Use a Period with Most Abbreviations**
 ◆ **Jan.** = January (Acronyms, such as IRS and CARE, do not require periods.)

■ **Question Marks End Direct Questions**
 ◆ Is Mary going to sell her house?

■ **Exclamation Points End Emphatic Statements**
 ◆ No cigars! Put that out now!

*The boldface text following the green-square bullets on this page does not require end punctuation because it is used as a **heading text**.

16 Other Punctuation

NOTES
Other punctuation notes marks have various functions.

- *Brackets*: **Enclose editorial comments inserted within quoted material.**
  - ◆ Machiavelli, the political pragmatist, argues that "princes **[or anyone in a position of power]** have accomplished most who paid little heed to keeping their promises."

- *Parentheses*: **Enclose supplemental information that is not necessary to the meaning of the sentence.**
  - ◆ There are three sections to a thoughtfully composed essay: **(1) the introduction, (2) the body, and (3) the conclusion.**
  - ◆ *Hamlet and the Law of Desire* **(1987)** suggests that Shakespeare's famous tragedy is about the traditional rite of passage all boys go through as they mature into men.

- *Em-dashes* **(typed as two hyphens with no space before, between, or after; or inserted as a symbol): Emphasize certain material within a sentence and indicate a dramatic pause.**

♦ I would suggest—**or should I say argue**—that all aspects of the present economy must be changed.

♦ Three members of the Board of Regents—**even the newly appointed member**—voted to reduce the education budget.

♦ Adam's mother—**a woman of high energy, intelligence, and wit**—always hosts the best parties.

■ *En-dashes*: **Separate combined-entity modifiers and are also used in number ranges.**
   ♦ The **mind–body** connection is powerful.
   ♦ The U.S Civil War (**1861–1865**) was one of the bloodiest war's in our nation's history.

■ *Hyphens*: **Join compounds and indicate line breaks—Some words are <u>always</u> hyphenated, so check the dictionary to be sure!**
   ♦ The **ill-fated** ship sank quickly.
   ♦ The **editor-in-chief** checked the final draft.
   ♦ The **player-King** delivered his lines expertly.
   ♦ **Anti-smoking** lobbyists roamed the halls of the government building.
   (Line-end hyphens break according to syllables.)

NOTES
Don't confuse dashes and hyphens!
-    hyphen
_   en-dash
—   em-dash

■ *Slashes*: **Indicate options and unindented lines of poetry.**
- ◆ Please use your book **and/or** a calculator.
- ◆ Good professors are true **teacher/scholars**.
- ◆ Many children recognize these famous lines: " 'Twas the night before Christmas, when all through the **house/Not** a creature was stirring, not even a mouse. . ."

■ *Ellipses (ellipsis points)*: **Indicate an omission from a direct quotation.**

NOTES
"Another **problem...** is *acid rain*...."
Three spaced periods indicate an omission within a quotation. Four spaced periods indicate an omission at the end of a direct quotation).

■ *Italics*: **Indicate titles of books, magazines, newspapers, long plays, poems, etc.**
- ◆ My sister can recite passages from *Walden*.
- ◆ *Newsweek* is my favorite news magazine.
- ◆ Daniel bought a copy of the *L.A. Times*.
- ◆ Professor Briggs can read *Paradise Lost* in Italian. *(Alternatively, you can underline titles.)*
- ◆ <u>Newsweek</u> is my favorite news magazine.

17 Writing: Word Choice & Diction

NOTES
Choice of words is the **first key** to good writing.

Nonstandard Language

■ **Slang** is unconventional language inappropriate for most college level writing.

Examples:
> **NOT** Evan was teed off when he bombed on the exam.
> **BUT** Evan was angry when he failed the exam.
> **(Use quotation marks for slang in formal essays.)**

■ **Colloquial language** is characterized by words and phrases common to spoken, informal English and characterizes immature writing.

Examples:
> **NOT** I ain't moving no time soon.
> **BUT** I am not moving anytime soon.
>
> **NOT** I don't get why parents fight all the time.
> **BUT** I do not understand why parents fight all the time.
> **(Colloquial language often includes contractions and grammatical errors.)**

■ **Regional language** is language specific to a geographic area of the country.

> *Examples:*
> ◆ We're fixing to go to a movie.
> **(The phrase "fixing to" is a Southern regionalism that means "getting ready" or "preparing.")**

■ **Pretentious language** is used in order to appear profound.

> *Examples:*
> **NOT** The Pater cogently recognizes the inherent scholastic integrity of a daily dose of newsy wit.
> **BUT** My father believes that reading a newspaper is an education in itself.

■ **Doublespeak**—from George Orwell's 1984— Refers to evasive language.

> *Examples:*
> ◆ Flight 743 made uncontrolled terrestrial contact. (**The sentence should read:** *Flight 743 crashed.*)
> ◆ The military spokesperson reported that several peacekeepers had been initiated against the enemy.
> **(The sentence should read: The military spokesperson reported that several bombs had been dropped on the enemy.)**

■ **Euphemisms** are words and phrases that substitute for words that are thought to be harsh or coarse.

Examples:
- ◆ We told the children that Aunt Mildred **had gone to her reward.** (she is dead)
- ◆ Uncle Filbert was taken away to a **correctional facility.** (jail)
- ◆ Carolyn thought she could save money by purchasing a **pre-owned car.** (used)

Technical Language

■ **Technical language** refers to the vocabulary specific to a profession or trade and which is familiar to those reading it.

Examples:
- ◆ If the **software overrides the default DIP settings**, the technician must initiate a new program sequence.
- ◆ During **pre-press**, imported color scans are separated into their **CMYK components**.

(Audience awareness is crucial when choosing technical language. Definitions and examples must be included for nontechnical readers.)

■ **Jargon** is technical language used without adequate explanations and directed toward a nontechnical audience in order to impress them.

Examples:
- ◆ In order to truly understand orchid culture, one must be familiar with **epiphytic**, **saprophytic** and **terrestrial** forms.

(The writer should define "epiphytic," "saprophytic" and "terrestrial.")

Biased Language
■ **Avoid using sexist language.**

Examples:

NOT Emily Dickinson is one of the most important **female poets** of the nineteenth century.

BUT Emily Dickinson is one of the most important **poets** of the nineteenth century.

NOT The **stewardess** will get you a drink.

BUT The **flight attendant** will get you a drink.

■ **Avoid using the generic "he" to refer to both sexes.**

Examples:

NOT A good student always begins **his** studying a few days before a major exam.

BUT A good student always begins **his or her** studying a few days before a major exam.

OR A good **student** always begins studying...

OR Good **students** always begin studying...

■ **Avoid using the generic "man" alone or as part of another word to refer to both sexes.**

Examples:

NOT The new computer desk is constructed of **man-made** materials.

BUT The new computer desk is constructed of **synthetic** materials.

NOT **Man** (or **mankind**) has made great leaps in computer technology over the past ten years.

BUT Great leaps in computer technology have been made over the past ten years.

■ Avoid occupational stereotypes.

Examples:

NOT A good secretary knows **her** way around complex computer systems.

BUT **A good secretary** can master complex computer systems.

NOT A respected lawyer will defend **his** client on the highest ethical grounds.

BUT **Respected lawyers** defend clients on the highest ethical grounds.

NOT Doctors and their **wives** donate heavily to reputable charities.

BUT Doctors and their **spouses** donate heavily to reputable charities.

NOT I wrote to the **chairman** of the committee.

BUT I wrote to the **chairperson** of the committee.

■ Rearrange sentences to remove singular pronouns.

Examples:

NOT A well-behaved child will not leave **her** toys on the floor.

BUT Well-behaved children will not leave **their** toys on the floor.

OR Well-behaved children will not leave toys on the floor.

(Most pronouns can be changed to plural forms.)

18 Writing: Exactness of Language

> **NOTES**
> Exact language is the **second key** to good writing.

Denotation/Connotation

■ A word's **denotation** refers to its *concrete, dictionary meaning.*

■ A word's **connotation** refers to what it *suggests or implies.*

Examples:
- ◆ Fred warned his children that bats bring evil.
- ◆ Fred watched as the bats flew out of the cave.

(In the first example, a negative connotation has been added to "bats" for effect.)

■ Use synonyms carefully to avoid connotation mistakes.

Examples:
- ◆ The diver was noted for his mighty breath.
- ◆ The diver was noted for his strong breath.

(Although "mighty" and "strong" can be synonyms, in this use they convey very different connotations.)

■ Consult a dictionary for the most specific information about a word.

Figurative Language

■ A simile expresses a comparison using either "like" or "as."
   ◆ Joan claims that her new daylily blooms shimmer like liquid gold.
   ◆ A Harley-Davidson motorcycle is as American as apple pie.

■ A metaphor expresses a subtle comparison without using either "like" or "as."
   "All the world's a stage and all the men and women merely players."
      —*William Shakespeare*

■ An extended metaphor develops over more than one sentence or paragraph.
   The economy can be compared to a living, breathing body, and money is the lifeblood of that body. In a healthy body, blood flows freely and unobstructed to all parts, nourishing them and removing any impurities that might harm the body. In a healthy economy, money also flows freely and abundantly to all sectors, nourishing the overall system and, in most instances, removing the impurities of poverty and hunger. If blood is obstructed in some way, the result can be disastrous. Strokes, heart attacks, dying limbs, etc. can ensue, ending in time and money-consuming health care or, worse, death. What we have seen in recent years is the stoppage of money flow from certain parts of the economy. As a result, the unemployment rate has risen, housing starts have

fallen, and, in general, a malaise has drifted over the nation. The question remains: How will we treat this serious lack of money flow, and will we be able to treat it in time to save the patient?

■ **Avoid mixed metaphors, which combine two or more incompatible comparisons.**

> *Examples:*
>
> **NOT** His creativity soars through the clouds but then falls like a soufflé.
>
> **BUT** His creativity soars into the sky only to get lost in the clouds.

■ **Personification is the transfer of human qualities or objects or ideas.**

"The car aimed ahead its lowered parking lights; under the hood purred the steady engine."

  —William Stafford

■ **Clichés are phrases that have become stale through overuse.**

> *Examples:*
>
> **NOT** The new car can stop on a dime.
> **BUT** The new car stops precisely.

■ **An idiom is a common phrase that has a fixed meaning independent of each word's separate definition.**

> *Examples:*
>
> ◆ Marcia cannot **agree with** John.
> ◆ Marcia and John cannot **agree on** a fixed plan.
> ◆ John cannot **agree to** such a proposal.
>
> **(Although the three phrases begin with "agree," the meanings are quite different.)**

■ **Use concrete and specific language to express your ideas clearly.**

Examples:

◆ John's teacher posted test grades outside her office.

VS.

◆ John's English professor posted the midterm exam grades outside her office in Turlington Hall.

(The first sentence is adequate, but the second provides more information.)

19 Writing: Conciseness of Language

NOTES

Concise language is the **third key** to good writing.

■ **Make every word count.**

Examples:

NOT Several actors **tried out in the auditions** for the role of Samuel.

BUT Several actors auditioned for the role of Samuel.

NOT Adam **called and said** he **could not** come over later to have dinner **with us.**

BUT Adam called. He's not coming for dinner.

(By employing an economy of words, the writer clarifies the meaning of each sentence.)

■ Remove unnecessary expletive constructions.

> *Examples:*
>
> **NOT** There were three ships that accompanied Christopher Columbus on his first voyage in 1492.
>
> **BUT** Three ships accompanied Christopher Columbus on his first voyage in 1492.
>
> **(An expletive is "there" or "it" followed by a form of the verb "to be." Expletive constructions weaken the sentence by placing the subject in a subordinate position.)**
>
> **(Sometimes an expletive is necessary to make a sentence meaningful: "It is raining.")**

■ Practice sentence combining to excise unnecessary words.

> *Examples:*
>
> **NOT** The sea was blue-gray. It spread out to the horizon in all directions. The surface was glassy and still.
>
> **BUT** The blue-gray sea, glassy and still, spread out to the horizon in all directions.
>
> **(The second sentence is short, succinct, and reads with a definite rhythm that is lacking in the first set of simple sentences.)**

■ **Repeat words or phrases carefully for clarity and emphasis.**

Examples:

> **NOT** John knew that Mark understood that the argument between John and Mark was not what John wanted.
>
> **BUT** John knew Mark understood that their argument was not what John wanted.

("John" must be repeated once for clarity.)

■ **Use commas and pronouns to reduce unnec-essary words.**

Examples:

> ◆ Knowledge is the goal for some students, career success for others, and wild parties for others.

(By removing "is the goal" from each phrase and adding commas, the writer successfully streamlines the sentence.)

> ◆ My father's success is amazing. He came from a poor family and had to work his way through college and law school.

(The pronouns replace "father.")

20 Writing: Know Your Audience

NOTES

Knowing your audience is the **fourth key** to good writing.

Checklist

- Is the audience an individual or a group? A specific group or a general group?
- What are the demographics of the audience? Age, gender, socioeconomic perspectives, religious and political attitudes?
- What does the audience know or need to know about the topic and are there misconceptions?
- What is the relationship between the writer and the audience? Boss, employee, student?
- How will the audience respond to the writing? With friendliness or hostility?
- Is specialized language necessary to the meaning of the writing? Should definitions be added for clarity?
- What does the writer want the audience to do? Is the writing an argumentative or persuasive piece? Is there adequate evidence, logic, and rationality present?

■ Should the writing be formal or informal? Where will it meet its audience? The classroom, a town meeting, a newspaper or journal?

■ Why is the audience reading the piece?

NOTES

The writer's responsibility is to be intelligible to the audience. If the audience does not understand the writing, it is the writer's fault.

21 Writing: Structure of Your Work

> **NOTES**
> Structure is the **fifth and final key** to good writing.

Unity

■ *Unity* refers to organizational patterns within paragraphs.

There have been many films about the high school experience. Most critics agree, however, that George Lucas' 1973 film, *American Graffiti,* established the genre. This agreement is not surprising, as the film's unique approach to period reconstruction, its use of the popular rock'n'roll of the era, and its narrative point of view combine into a telling portrait of the social alternatives available to teenagers in 1962. More recently, Amy Heckerling and Richard Linklater have directed their own versions of the high school rite of passage. Heckerling's *Fast Times at Ridgemont High (1982)* and Linklater's *Dazed and Confused (1993,* but set in 1976) present conflicting images of the American high school student in the early years of the last quarter of the twentieth century.

Examples:
- ◆ Each sentence relates to the other sentences.
- ◆ Each sentence contains the same grammatical elements.

Balance

■ *Balance* **refers to sentence structure within paragraphs.**

In 1900, during the Great Exposition in Paris, Henry Adams wandered into the hall of dynamos and stood transfixed before a force he knew would reshape the world. This simple act of acknowledgment produced such powerful emotions that Adams would be haunted until his death with the paradox of "The Dynamo and the Virgin." Although Adams could appreciate the knowledge of physics necessary to construct a dynamo, he could also envision a danger within the dynamo itself: "Before the end, one began to pray to it; inherited instinct taught the natural expression of man before the silent and infinite force." The dynamo would become the new religion of the twentieth century.

—*Michael Briggs*

Examples:

♦ The writer varies sentence length to hold his reader's attention.

♦ The addition of a quotation from the source text adds legitimacy to the essay.

♦ The last sentence, a simple sentence, adds force and energy to the longer, complex sentences that constitute the body of the paragraph.

♦ By not mentioning the dynamo by name until the end of the second sentence, the writer effectively increases the tension within the paragraph.

♦ The concluding sentence includes a hook— the new religion—that will draw the reader into the essay.

Cohesion

■ *Cohesion* **refers to paragraph development within the essay.**

For Adams, the virgin suggested both the infinite power of such a dynamic force and the religious symbolism of the virgin who was the idealized protector of a fallible human race. What would happen if this sacred symbol of fertility, power, and humanity were eclipsed by the dynamo? Mary, in her dual role of human and virgin mother of Jesus, became a link between humanity and a spiritual universe of perfection and "kindness."

Examples:

◆ The second paragraph continues the theme established in the first paragraph, and it begins the development of the issue of religion as it ties the dynamo and the virgin together.

◆ Subsequent paragraphs will continue this theme while developing pertinent topics.

Parallelism

■ *Parallelism* **refers to specific writing strategies that emphasize through repetition.**

American society is at an important crossroads in its cultural development. *It must not allow* drug abuse to determine its future. *It cannot allow* violence to determine its future. And *it should not allow* special interest groups to determine its future.

Examples:
- ◆ The three parallel sentences work together because they build on a common topic—problems in American society—and include similar grammatical elements.
- ◆ The overall style of the selection stems from its verb progression within the sentences.

(Do not overuse parallelism. It provides a distinct stylistic effect, but it can also clutter writing.)

22 Composing an Essay

> **NOTES**
> Having learned the five keys to good writing
> [refer to chapters 17–21], you are now ready
> to write your own essay.

Establishing Purpose

Purpose Can Be Divided into Four Categories

■ *Narration*: **A narrative essay tells a story by relating a sequence of events.**

◆ An essay narrating events that led Martin Luther to post his 95 theses on the door of the castle church at Wittenburg on October 31, 1517.

◆ An essay narrating events that led to the stock market crash in 1929.

■ *Description*: **A descriptive essay focuses on an event, a person, an object, or a setting and depends upon details and images.**

◆ An essay describing Claude Monet's lily pond and flower gardens at his home in Giverny.

◆ A descriptive essay looking at the architectural styles in St. Augustine, Florida.

■ *Explanation*: **An explanatory essay (an exposition) explains, analyzes, or interprets an issue.**

- ◆ An exposition on the effects of the Conservative Right in the Republican party.
- ◆ An analysis of governmental AIDS funding over the past decade.
- ◆ An essay interpreting speeches at a national political convention in light of specific socio-economic information.

■ *Argumentation*: **An argumentative essay attempts to persuade readers to take some action or convince them of the writer's position.**
- ◆ An essay designed to alert citizens to the danger of urban crime and get them to start neighborhood watch programs.
- ◆ An essay designed to convince readers that capital punishment does not serve a social need.

NOTES
It is permissible, even desirable, to include elements of more than one purpose category in an essay, as long as there is a dominant purpose guiding the essay.

Establishing a Pattern
An Essay Can Be Divided into Three Distinct Parts

■ *The Introduction*: **One or two paragraphs that introduce the topic to the reader.**
The introduction includes the thesis statement, a single sentence that states a topic and an opinion about the topic.

■ *The Body*: **Several paragraphs that present the evidence in an orderly manner.**
Each paragraph in the body organizes around a topic sentence that relates to the thesis statement.

■ *The Conclusion*: **Usually no more than one paragraph that brings a tone of finality to the essay.**
The conclusion includes a restatement of the thesis statement and touches on the main ideas presented in the body of the essay.

Five-Paragraph Essay

■ *Introduction*: **One paragraph in length moving from general sentences to a specific thesis statement as the final sentence.**

■ *Body*: **Three paragraphs in length with the emphasis on specific pieces of evidence that support the thesis.**

■ *Conclusion*: **One paragraph moving from a specific restatement of the thesis statement to a general statement of finality.**
This classic form is often used in freshman writing courses to introduce the essay. It is however, structurally limited for longer topics or research papers and should not serve as a model for all academic writing. Instead, the beginning writer should use its essential elements—a clear thesis and concrete supports—as a basis for more complex essay formats.

Discovering a Topic

■ A Topic Is a Specific Refining of a Subject

Subject—Art (much too broad)
Topic—Impressionism (too broad)
Topic—Claude Monet (still too broad)
Topic—Monet's art and his garden (workable)

■ Certain Questions Can Help a Writer Narrow Down a Subject Appropriately

◆ What am I interested in writing about?
◆ Do I have special knowledge in a particular area?
◆ What do I want to learn about?
◆ How much time do I have?

■ The Key to Successfully Narrowing a Topic Lies in Moving from Generalities to Specific Information

A writer might wish to deal with a specific group of paintings—no more than two or three—and examine Monet's artistic style as it was influenced by his approach to the landscape around his home in Giverny.

Building Paragraphs

■ Examples & Illustrations

Monet planted his pond with several varieties of hardy water lilies and surrounded the pond with grasses, poppies, irises, and antique roses.

■ Definition

A multimedia presentation is similar to traditional business presentations except that it relies upon visuals such as pictures, slides, and films as well as audio to augment text-based material.

■ **Analog**
Martin Luther's decision to post his 95 theses was, for the Catholic church, tantamount to Satan's fall from grace.

■ **Comparison & Contrast**
Although both St. Augustine, Florida and Williamsburg, Virginia represent colonial urban centers, their styles of architecture hint at vastly different cultural histories.

■ **Cause & Effect**
Many historians relate the Great Depression of the 1930's with the stock market crash in 1929, but evidence of an industrial slump predates the crash by at least four years.

■ **Classification & Division**
Of the many orchids popular in the U.S., three species constitute sixty percent of all sales: Cattleya, Cymbidium, and Paphiopedilum.

■ **Process Analysis**
Establishing a freshwater aquarium involves five simple steps that, when accomplished, will result in a beautiful environment for fish.

NOTES
Most writers incorporate elements of more than one development strategy while, at the same time, establishing a dominant paragraph development.

Developing a Thesis

■ **An Effective Thesis Statement Presents a Topic and an Opinion About That Topic**

Examples:

◆ Films about American high schools are interesting.

(This thesis statement lacks adequate detail. The topic—films about American high schools—is too broad, and the opinion—they are interesting—lacks authority and strength.)

Examples:

◆ Richard Linklater's *Dazed and Confused* and Amy Heckerling's *Fast Times* present conflicting images of the American high school student.

(The revised thesis statement employs precise details and concrete language designed to entice the potential reader.)

■ **Statements of Fact or Purpose Should Not Be Confused with Thesis Statements.**

Examples:

◆ *Dazed and Confused* and *Fast Times* are two films about American high school students.

(The statement of fact does not require development or evidence to back it up.)

Examples:

◆ I am going to prove that *Dazed and Confused* is a better film than *Fast Times*.

(The statement of purpose is similar to the thesis statement, but it lacks style and substance and is too broad.)

Generating Material

■ Ask the Reporter's Questions

Examples:

◆ Who? What? Where? When? Why? How?

(Applying these reporter's questions to a topic can lead to more ideas and places for information.)

■ Brainstorming

Writers use brainstorming (free association) when they know something about a topic. They simply list ideas in no particular order and without taking time to censor their ideas.

■ Clustering

Clustering is similar to brainstorming but includes a definite organizational pattern. The main idea is placed in a circle in the middle of a piece of paper. Lines radiate out from the main idea to more circles that enclose relevant ideas. The process is repeated with more ideas until the basic approach appears.

■ Freewriting

This process allows writers to investigate a topic through short, timed writing exercises. A writer should allow five to ten minutes for each period of freewriting and should not stop writing during that time. Writer's block is not an excuse here.

If nothing comes to mind about a topic, the writer should simply write "I don't know what to write."

■ Journaling

Similar to freewriting, journaling allows a writer to explore issues related to a topic in a non-threatening environment. No one will see the journal, and the writer can feel free to record thoughts and observations that often lead to a more reasoned and insightful approach to an essay.

■ Research

Doing research on a topic is the classic way to generate usable material for an essay. However, research need not be the formal type of work necessary for a lengthy analytical paper. Research can extend to first-hand observation or interviews with people who have pertinent knowledge. The key is to keep adequate and careful notes for later use when composing the essay.

The Outline

■ **An outline organizes material in a logical sequence and allows the writer to place subtopics and evidence in the most appropriate places. (It can be created at any time during or after composing the essay to make a logical check of organization.)**

Informal Outline

Working Title: A Comparison of Two Teenager Films

Purpose: To contrast rite-of-passage themes in *Fast Times* and *Dazed and Confused.*

Thesis: *Fast Times* and *Dazed and Confused* present contrasting views of the teenage rite of passage during the last decades of the twentieth century.

1. Introduction
2. Body: A comparison of how the two films approach social alternatives available to high school seniors during the decades following the turbulent sixties.
   a. Adults versus teenagers.
   b. Rules and rites of passage.
   c. Teens and the work world.
   d. Social implications of the year the film was produced.
3. Conclusion

Formal Outline

The formal outline is similar to the informal outline except that it is written in complete sentences and each category is divided into at least two subcategories. It follows the traditional formal outline pattern, including the category indicators below.

I
  A.
  B.
    1.
    2.
      a.
      b.
        (1)
        (2)
          (a)
          (b)
            i.
            ii.

The First Draft

■ **Experienced writers begin their first draft after gathering and organizing sufficient material for the essay.**

- ◆ View both films at least two times in order to become thoroughly familiar with their content.
- ◆ Read selected film reviews.
- ◆ Brainstorm various issues that arise from the films.
- ◆ Employ other techniques to generate material such as journaling or discussing the films with friends.

■ **DO NOT assume that the first draft will be the final draft. Prudent writers allow time to work on several drafts of an essay, but many beginning writers procrastinate until the night before it is due.**

- ◆ While writing the first draft, do not edit extensively. The purpose is to get words and ideas onto paper.
- ◆ Overwrite the first draft, even to the point of repeating ideas. It is easier to cut away excess words than to pad insufficient writing.
- ◆ Use freewriting techniques to explore side issues that might warrant developing into significant sections of the essay.

■ **When the first draft is finished, leave the material alone for a short period of time before working on a second draft.**

- ◆ The first draft does not follow any particular order. Beginning writers should focus on writing those sections they feel comfortable with. Most writers begin with the body of the essay before they approach the introduction or conclusion.

◆ During the time away from the draft, the writer might wish to review important information, such as viewing the films another time or re-reading notes taken early in the pre-writing process.

Revision Techniques

■ **During the revision process, writers become more editorial in their approach, looking at the large elements first.**

◆ Is the topic well focused?In the essay, the writer wishes to show how there is a sense of community present in *Dazed and Confused* that is not present in *Fast Times*.

◆ Is the thesis statement clear?The thesis—the underlying theme—establishes that the two movies present conflicting images of American teenagers and their social alternatives.

◆ Are there adequate examples and are they clear? By focusing on specific elements in the films—the opening scenes (e.g. the ticket scalping), the dialogue, etc.; the writer provides support for the essay that increases its effectiveness.

◆ Are the paragraphs effective?Originally, the third and fourth paragraphs were one paragraph. By separating it, the writer shifts smoothly from rules to rituals to a discussion of the opening scenes, which works well with the overall development of the essay.

◆ Is the purpose of the essay accomplished?The combined effect of supportable, concrete examples and a strong pattern of development is that of a solid, well-written freshman composition. The writer does accomplish his task of illustrating commonalities, or the lack thereof, in the two films.

■ **By applying these questions to a rough draft, the writer can revise more effectively.**

■ **When larger elements of an essay have been revised, smaller elements can be tackled.**
- ◆ Do the sentences work well? Is there a balance of simple and complex sentences?
- ◆ Are there adequate transitions between sentences and paragraphs? Is the language appropriate?
- ◆ Are there excess words or redundant ideas that can be removed from the essay?

The Finished Essay
Dazed and Confused At Ridgemont High: A Comparison of Two Films

There have been many films about the high school experience. Most critics agree, however, that George Lucas' 1973 film, *American Graffiti,* established the genre. This agreement is not surprising, as the film's unique approach to period reconstruction, its use of the popular rock'n'roll of the era, and its narrative point of view combine into a telling portrait of the social alternatives available to teenagers in 1962. More recently, Amy Heckerling and Richard Linklater have directed their own versions of the high school rite of passage. Heckerling's *Fast Times at Ridgemont High* (1982) and Linklater's *Dazed and Confused* (1993, but set in 1976) present conflicting images of the American high school student in the early years of the last quarter of the twentieth century.

One element that remains fairly constant throughout the various teenager films is the adversarial relationship between teens and adults, particularly parents and teachers. The school dance scene in *American Graffiti* in which Laurie (Cindy Williams) and Steve (Ron Howard) are asked to move apart illustrates this point. Even though Steve has already graduated, the teacher tries to force him to obey what Steve feels are antiquated rules of behavior. Similarly, students in *Fast Times at Ridgemont High* must deal with the authoritarian personality of Mr. Hand (Ray Walston), and the football players in *Dazed and Confused,* especially Pink (Jason London), must contend with the coach's anti-drug campaign. Interestingly, though, most students in *Fast Times* seem to acquiesce to Hand's rather draconian teaching methods. Students in *American Graffiti* and *Dazed and Confused* rebel against authority.

Rules and rites of passage also differ between *Dazed and Confused* and *Fast Times.* For instance, much of Linklater's film centers on the hazing that takes place as the incoming freshmen encounter their senior tormentors. Ironically, what arises from the embarrassing and sometimes extreme hazing is a sense of community among the students that is lacking in Heckerling's film. Later, as Pink introduces Mitch to his friends at a local bar, it becomes evident that Mitch is being accepted into the larger group of high school students. Such comraderie does not exist in *Fast Times.* Instead, Brad (Judge Reinhold) and Stacy (Jennifer Jason Leigh) seem more interested in emulating adult pursuits, especially working and earning money.

A comparison of the two films' opening scenes will illustrate the fundamental differences between the way the teenagers view the world. *Dazed and Confused* begins at school with several students smoking marijuana and, in general, "hanging out." *Fast Times* begins in a mall with teenagers going to work. In particular, Damone (Robert Romanus) is trying to scalp tickets to a concert, which is, apparently, his major form of income. While the teens in *Dazed and Confused* spend time going to parties and planning their next party, teens in *Fast Times* spend time at work.

At one point, Mike (Adam Goldberg) remarks, "What we need are some good-old, worthwhile, visceral experiences." And they do. Much of *Dazed and Confused* is about the visceral experience of high school, drug use, parties, budding romance, fights, and above all, the visceral experience of bonding among young people that is missing in *Fast Times,* as is the relative innocence that radiates from Linklater's characters. With the exception of Spicoli (Sean Penn), the "surfer dude," pot-smoking teen, Heckerling's characters do not have much fun. They act out a fantasy of adult behavior replete with unfulfilling sex, money and cars, but they do not have the freedom of adulthood, just the responsibilities. When Brad takes Stacy, his sister, to have an abortion, the audience feels acutely the darkness of their situation. On the other hand, Pink *(Dazed and Confused)* ultimately refuses to sign the anti-drug statement and drives off into the sunrise of another day, laughing. Brad is unhappy because his adult fantasy is just that, a fantasy. Pink experiences the reality of being young and relatively free of responsibility.

One of the most subtle relationships in *Fast Times* exists between Mr. Hand and Spicoli. Hand has always thought that the problem with teenagers stems from their drug use, but apparently, Spicoli is one of only a few teens in the film who uses drugs. Later, Spicoli remarks: "All I need are some tasty waves, cool buzz, and I'm fine." The importance of Spicoli's philosophy lies in his attitude rather than his choice of activities. Spicoli acts like a time traveler from *Dazed and Confused* who finds himself among teenagers who act more like miniature adults with full-size neuroses than teenagers having fun. Perhaps Hand recognizes Spicoli's "sincerity" and respects him for it.

It is possible to view *Dazed and Confused* and *Fast Times* as sociological representations of their times. *Dazed and Confused* portrays a rebellious generation—similar to *American Graffiti*—that draws its energy and power from its sense of community. *Fast Times at Ridgemont High* hints at a generation that has sacrificed its sense of community in order to play at being adults. In either case, however, we see the enduring theme of teenagers dealing with their encroaching maturity the best way they know how.

Manuscript Form

■ Typewritten Essays

◆ A good quality, medium-weight white paper (25% cotton) is best for typewritten essays. Do not use erasable bond or onion skin paper.

◆ Use a black ribbon and clean the typing element.

◆ Type on one side of the paper only and double space. Double space indented quotations.

◆ Use white-out to correct errors, but retype pages that contain numerous errors.

◆ Use correct spacing after marks of punctuation.
  • two spaces at the end of a sentence
  • two spaces after a colon
  • one space after a comma or semicolon

◆ Fasten pages with a paper clip or staple, depending on the professor's recommendation.

■ Computer-Generated Essays

◆ Make sure that the computer formats the essay to normal manuscript margins (approximately one inch on all sides). Check with the professor before using right justification.

◆ Final copies should be printed on a letter or near-letter quality printer.

◆ Keep extra printer cartridges on hand to ensure a clean final draft.

◆ Use good quality, medium-weight white paper.

◆ Remove any perforated strips and separate pages.

◆ Use a paper clip or staple to secure pages.

■ General Formatting Rules

◆ Display essay information on a separate title page or on the first page of the essay in the upper left margin, in the format shown here:

Adam Hunter

Professor Michael Briggs

Freshman Composition 1101-002

October 21, 2005

◆ Center titles, but do not italicize or underline original titles. Capitalize important words. Do not use a cover title page unless your professor requests one.

◆ Indent paragraphs three to five spaces and double that amount for indented quotations (including poetry and prose).

◆ Use Arabic numerals and number all pages in upper right margin beginning with first page.

Proofreading

■ Always Proofread Your Essay Before Submitting It

◆ Check for spelling with a spell-check or a dictionary. Try reading the essay backwards to catch spelling errors.

◆ Check for grammatical errors, especially those involving comma usage.

◆ Have a friend or classmate proofread the essay.

◆ Keep a copy of the essay in case something happens to the original.

23 Commonly Misspelled Words

> **NOTES**
> Use this index of common misspellings whenever you're writing.

D

debt
deceased
decision
definitely
definitive
delegate
delicious
dependent
despair
desperately
despise
diaphragm
difference
disappear
disease
disguise
dissatisfied
duplicate
dysfunction

E

eager
effervescent
efficient
eligible
eliminate
emanate
embarrass
eminent
environment
equipped
erroneous
exaggerate
exceed
excessive
exercise
exhaust
extraordinary

F

fallacy
famous
fascinate
fatigue
February
fluorescent
foliage
foreclose
foreclosure
fulfill

G

gauge
genealogy
glamorous
glamour
gnaw
government
gracious
grateful
guarantee
guidance
guilty
gymnasium

H

handkerchief
harass
hemorrhage
hindrance
horrible
hypocrisy

I

identical
important
inadvertent
incredible
independence
inevitable
infinitesimal
inimitable
initiation
installation
interrupt
iridescent
irrelevant
irresistible
isthmus

J

jealous
jeopardize
judgment
justifiable

K

kitchen
knowledge

L

laboratory
language
larynx
league
library
license
licorice
liquefy
literature
logarithm
luxury

M

magnificent
maintenance
maneuver
mathematics
measure
mediocre
memento
merchandise
miscellaneous
mischievous
miserable
missionary
misspell
momentous
mortgage

N

naive
naturally
necessary
negotiate
neighbor
niece
noticeable
notoriety
nuisance

O

obedience
obsess
occurred
omitted
ophthalmology
optician
optometrist

P

pamphlet
paradise
parallel
parliament
pastime
pejorative
perceive
permanent
pharaoh
plaid
plateau
playwright

pneumonia
porcelain
possession
possible
potato
potatoes
precedence
preliminary
prerogative
privilege
probably
professor
pronunciation
ptomaine
publicly
pursue
pursuing

Q

qualify
quantify
quantity
questionnaire
quotient

R

rarefy
receipt
receive
recess
recipe
recommend
referred

reign
relevant
reminiscence
remittance
rendezvous
repetition
reservoir
restaurant
rhythm
ridiculous

S

sacrilegious
salary
scissors
secretary
seize
separately
sergeant
several
siege
significance
similar
sincerely
soldier
soliloquy
statute
succeed
sufficient
summarize
supersede
synonymous

T

technique
temperament
temperance
therefore
thief
threshold
tobacco
tomato
tomatoes
tomorrow
tournament
tourniquet
tragedy
tranquilizer
transferred
truly
Tuesday
tuition
typical

U

unanimous
unconscious
unfortunately
unique
usable
usually
utensil

V

vacation
vaccinate

vacuum
valuable
vengeance
villain
violence
visible
visitor
volume

W

wander
warrant
Wednesday
weird
whether
wholly
width
withhold
worthwhile

Y

yesterday
yield

Z

zephyr

24 Frequently Misused/ Confused Words

NOTES
Use this glossary of misused/confused words
whenever you're writing.

A

ability/capacity: Often used interchangeably;
ability refers to a learned/acquired skill, **capacity** to
the potential to learn or acquire a skill (*"He has the
capacity to do calculus."*)

accept/except: Accept: to take in or agree to;
except: omission or exclusion

adapt/adopt: Adapt: to adjust to a particular
situation, use, area; **adopt:** to accept and use as
one's own

adapted/suitable (suited): Adapted: made
suitable for a particular use; **suitable/suited**: ready
for use

adjacent/contiguous: Adjacent: next to;
contiguous: touching and, more specifically, part of a
continuing thing. *New York is **adjacent** to New Jersey;
the eastern shoreline of the U.S. is **contiguous.***

adopted/adoptive: A thing, person, idea, etc., is **adopted** by an **adoptive** person, organization, etc.

adverse/averse: **Adverse:** hostile, unfavorable; **averse:** reluctant; *"I am **averse** to doing something that may cause an adverse reaction."*

affect/effect: **Affect:** to influence; used most commonly as a verb; **effect:** to accomplish or cause; most commonly used as a noun; the differences are subtle; **effect** is increasingly accepted for both

aggravate/agitate: **Aggravate:** to make worse; **agitate:** to stir up or annoy

aisle/isle: **Aisle:** a straight path, for example, between two rows of seats in a theater; **isle:** a small island

allude/refer: One **alludes** to something indirectly, but **refers** to it directly

allusion/illusion: An **allusion** is a reference to something; an **illusion** is a false appearance

already/all ready: **Already:** previously; **all ready:** completely prepared

altar/alter: **Altar:** A place where religious rites are performed; **alter:** to change

alternately/alternatively: **Alternately:** one *after* the other; **alternatively:** one *or* the other

amend/emend: Although both mean to modify/improve, change, or revise, **emend** almost always refers to written texts

amiable/amicable/amenable: All refer to friendliness, but only a person can be **amiable;** agreements, moods, situations, are **amicable;** neither should be confused with **amenable:** willing to listen or agree

amid/among/between: We are generally **amid** something when we are *in the middle* (figuratively) of a large number; we are **among** quantifiable numbers; and we are only between two things; (*"I was **among** the six people who got lost **amid** the trees **between** the two farms."*)

amoral/immoral: **Amoral** is not knowing what is moral; **immoral** is knowing what's moral, and defying it

anxious/eager: **Anxious** implies worry or unease; **eager** offers a sense of happy anticipation

apology/excuse: An **apology** is an admission of wrong; an **excuse** is an attempt to justify the wrong act

appraise/apprise: **Appraise:** evaluate, set a price on; **apprise:** inform

as/like: This distinction is rapidly disappearing; **as:** in accordance with what is expected; **like:** something that is similar to something else

ascent/assent: **Ascent:** to move upward; **assent:** to agree

assay/essay: **Assay:** test; **essay:** a short paper

avenge/revenge/vengeance: Often used interchangeably, there is a notable distinction: a wrong done to someone else is **avenged; revenge** seeks retribution for a wrong (real or imagined) to oneself; in both cases, **vengeance** is taken

avoid/evade: **Avoid:** to keep away from or prevent; **evade:** to escape

B

bail/bale: Unless you're making something into a large bundle or **bale**, the word is almost always **bail**

bazaar/bizarre: **Bazaar:** a marketplace or similar area/activity where diverse items are for sale; **bizarre:** weird, strange

beside/besides: **Beside:** next to, at the side of; **besides:** except, in addition to, other than

biannual/biennial: **Biannual:** twice a year; **biennial:** every two years

blatant/flagrant: **Blatant:** loud, obvious, and "noisy" in a very public way; **flagrant:** outrageous

breach/breech: A **breach** is a "violation" of something such as a breach of faith or a crack in a wall; a **breech** is the back of the bore in a gun, rifle, etc.

breath/breathe/breadth: **Breath:** A noun; the act of inhaling and exhaling; **breathe:** a verb; to inhale and exhale; never confuse with **breadth**, meaning width or scope

bring/take: Use **bring** to carry something from a farther place to a nearer place. Use **take** to carry something from a near place to a farther place.

C

Calvary/cavalry: One of the more common misspellings, **Calvary** (always capitalized) is the geographic location of the crucifixion of Jesus; *cavalry* refers to soldiers on horseback and, more recently, in tanks

can/may: Another distinction that is rapidly disappearing; **can** refers to the ability to do something; **may** to permission

canvas/canvass: **Canvas:** the coarse material used for sails, tents, etc.; **canvass:** to circulate in a neighborhood or on the phone, to solicit support/information, etc.

capital/capitol: With an "a" it's the city where the seat of government resides; with an "o" it's the *building* where the government meets

censor/censure: **Censor:** repress/delete; **censure:** rebuke harshly

cereal/serial: **Cereal:** grain, breakfast food; **serial:** continuous actions as part of a whole

chaff/chafe: Chaff: tease; **chafe:** irritate by rubbing; (**chaff** also means the waste material discarded when processing wheat)

childish/childlike: Although both mean, essentially, acting like a child, **childish** bears a negative connotation implying lack of maturity, while **childlike** implies the positive aspects of being mature yet retaining one's youthful outlook

choral/chorale: Choral refers to the chorus/choir; **chorale** is a noun referring to a hymn or other sacred music

chord/cord: A **chord** is a combination of musical notes played together; *all* other instances use **cord**, as in string/rope, etc.; because of the musical association "vocal **chord**" is often used for the anatomical structure but it is "vocal **cord**"

clamber/clamor: Clamber: climb, usually implying awkwardness; **clamor:** noise

climactic/climatic: Climactic: the climax; **climatic:** pertaining to the weather

coarse/course: Coarse: crude, rough in texture; **course:** path or plan of travel, or a class or series of classes

colonel/kernel: Colonel: military rank; **kernel:** an edible seed, or, figuratively, the core of an idea

compare/contrast: One **compares** the totality of one thing/person with another; one **contrasts** only the differences (compare *with*; contrast *to*)

complacent/complaisant: **Complacent:** smug, self-satisfied; **complaisant:** eager to please

complement/compliment: **Complement:** to make complete, to make better or "perfect"; **compliment:** an expression of praise/politeness

comptroller/controller: Another distinction that is disappearing; **comptroller** refers to a financial officer in a company/government, etc.; **controller** refers to anybody/thing that controls

confidant/confident (confidante): **Confidant:** someone told confidential information; **confident:** self-assured; **confidante** refers to a female confidant, and is rapidly falling into disuse

connote/denote: **Connote** implies/suggests; **denote** expresses specifically

consistency/constancy: **Consistency:** an agreement within a set of actions, argument, etc.; **constancy:** faithfulness; note: **consistency** also refers to a measure of thickness

contagious/infectious: **Contagious** diseases spread by direct contact; those that are **infectious** spread through the air

contemptible/contemptuous: A despicable action is **contemptible;** the action is noted with a **contemptuous,** or displeased attitude

continual/continuous: **Continual** activities occur over a period of time, but are not constant: (*"I am continually telling my kids to clean up their room."*) **Continuous** activities are constant: (*"The noise was continuous."*)

convince/persuade: A person is **convinced** of the correctness of an idea and **persuaded** to take action

council/counsel: **Council:** a body of people who make decisions; **counsel:** to give advice and, in law, the lawyer who gives that advice

credible/creditable/credulous: Often incorrectly used interchangeably; **credible:** simply, believable; **creditable:** praiseworthy; **credulous:** gullible

D

debar/disbar: Anyone can be **debarred** or excluded; **disbarred** is used only for lawyers whose credentials have been removed

deceased/diseased: **Deceased:** to be dead; **diseased:** to have an illness

definite/definitive: **Definite:** something precise and specific; **definitive:** something that is the perfect example, beyond any challenge; often used hyperbolically or figuratively

defuse/diffuse: **defuse:** to make less harmful or to reduce the tension of a situation; **diffuse:** scattered or poorly organized (use as a verb and an adjective)

delusion/illusion: A subtle difference—a **delusion** is a false *belief*, an **illusion** is a false *perception* (*"Because she was under the **delusion** that he was a kind person, she formed the **illusion** that he was handsome, as well."*)

deprecate/depreciate: **Deprecate:** to disapprove of; **depreciate:** to make smaller; *however,* when someone makes him/herself appear "smaller" out of modesty, *self-deprecating* is used rather than *self-depreciating* (this is considered acceptable by most dictionaries)

desert/dessert: **Desert:** a very hot place; **dessert:** the good stuff at the end of a meal; the phrase "just deserts" has little to do with either of these, and means "what one deserves"

deviate/digress: One **deviates** from a standard or a course of action; one **digresses** from the main topic in a conversation or a piece of writing

dilate/contract: **Dilate:** grow larger: **contract:** grow smaller

disapprove/disprove: Disapprove: find unfavorable; **disprove:** show to be false

disburse/disperse: Disburse: pay out; **disperse:** scatter

discreet/discrete: Discreet: circumspect, careful; **discrete:** separate

disinterested/uninterested: Disinterested: impartial; **uninterested:** not caring

dissent/descent: Dissent: to disagree with, usually strongly; **descent:** come down from

distinct/distinguished: Distinct: unmistakably separate from; **distinguished:** eminent, praiseworthy

dyeing/dying: Dyeing: the act of coloring something with dye; **dying:** the process of becoming dead

E

earthy/earthly: Earthy: in common use: vulgar, coarse, realistic ("down to earth"), or, more specifically, soil, land, etc.; **earthly:** of the Earth, as opposed to of the heavens in either religious or "outer space" terminology

ecology/environment: The **environment** applies to the entire area in which something exists; **ecology** is the interaction between different components of the environment

e.g./i.e.: Often mistakenly interchanged, **e.g.** means "for example" and precedes the actual example(s); **i.e.** means "that is," or "that is to say," and adds a new thought or corollary to its precedent

elegy/eulogy: **Elegy:** a song/poem for the dead; **eulogy:** a prose statement for the dead

elicit/illicit: **Elicit:** bring forth, especially a comment or response; **illicit:** illegal

elusive/illusive: **Elusive:** hard to grasp, comprehend, or identify; **illusive:** illusory or deceptive

emigrate/immigrate: **Emigrate:** to leave from; **immigrate:** to go/come to

eminent/imminent: **Eminent:** prominent, distinguished; **imminent:** due at any moment

empathy/sympathy: **Empathy** is *sharing* another's feelings, often because one has experienced similar ones; **sympathy** is *understanding* and agreeing with those feelings

enervate/invigorate: **Enervate:** to weaken; **invigorate:** the opposite of enervate; to give life and energy

enormity/enormousness: While **enormousness** refers to anything great or large, **enormity** is reserved *only* for large or great evil

ensure/insure: Generally interchangeable, but when referring to insurance policy coverage, only **insure** should be used

entomology/etymology: Entomology: the study of bugs (insects); **etymology:** the study of words

enviable/envious: Something **enviable** is desirable; one who is **envious** is jealous

epitaph/epigraph: Both are inscriptions; an **epitaph** is reserved for a tombstone, while an **epigraph** usually appears on a building, but can also appear in literature as a quotation used to establish a theme

equable/equitable: Equable: uniform, even, and, by extension, calm, not easily disturbed; **equitable:** fair/just/even-handed

essentially/substantially: Something that is **essential** is vital to the whole; something **substantial** may comprise a large amount of the whole, but may not be vital

exceedingly/excessively: Exceedingly: extremely, to a large degree; **excessively:** too much

exceptional/exceptionable: Exceptional: out of the ordinary; **exceptionable:** objectionable

explicit/implicit: Explicit: clear; **implicit:** hinted at

extended/extensive: **Extended:** stretched out, lengthened; **extensive:** vast, large

F

farther/further: **Farther:** physical distance; **further:** extent or degree (moreover additionally are synonymous with extent or degree further)

fatal/fateful: **Fatal:** to result in or cause death; **fateful:** having a major consequence

faze/phase: **Faze:** bother; **phase:** an aspect of the whole

fewer/less: **Fewer** refers to specific numbers; *"10 items or fewer"*; **less** refers to unquantifiable things; *"less than fully satisfied"*; (fewer is *plural*; less is *singular*)

fiancé/fiancée: **fiancé:** male partner in an engaged couple; **fiancée:** female partner in an engaged couple

final/finale: Use **final** to mean last/end, etc.; **finale** is a noun, and should be reserved for the "final" piece, especially of a musical performance

flair/flare: **Flair:** with taste and style; **flare:** a flash of light or outburst

flammable/inflammable/non-flammable: Contrary to the rules of grammar, both **flammable** and inflammable mean capable of burning; **non-flammable** (or *non-inflammable*) items will not burn

flaunt/flout: Often mistakenly used interchangeably, **flaunt** means to display in a grand manner, while **flout** means to show contempt for

flounder/founder: Flounder: to thrash about in confusion; **founder:** to sink (note that the same words have different meanings when used as nouns)

forbear/forebear: Forbear: to hold back, to be patient with; **forebear:** an ancestor

forego/forgo: Forego: go ahead of; **forgo:** pass up on

foreword/forward: Foreword: introduction to a section before the main text (technically, written by someone other than the author; otherwise it is a preface); **forward:** in a direction ahead

former/latter: Former: the first named of two things; **latter:** the last named of two things

formally/formerly: Formally: with proper consideration of "form," properly, legally; **formerly:** once, but no longer

forth/fourth: Forth: forward, ahead; **fourth:** the next in sequence after third

fortuitous/fortunate: While **fortunate** is usually associated with *good* luck; **fortuitous** applies to any "chance" happening, good or bad

fulsome/abundant: **Fulsome:** grotesquely *overdone;* **abundant:** lots of

G

gibe/jibe/jib: **Gibe:** to make fun of; **jibe:** a nautical term for changing direction, or slang for agreement; **jib:** a triangular sail on the front of a ship

good/well: **Good** is an adjective and should be used with a noun/pronoun—it also has a moral connotation; **well** is an adverb and has no moral implication

grandiloquent/eloquent: **Grandiloquent:** using pompous or overblown language; **eloquent:** moving, clear, and precise

H

hangar/hanger: A **hangar** houses airplanes; a **hanger** is used for clothing

hardy/hearty: **Hardy:** strong, healthy, bold; **hearty:** cordial and effusive

hoard/horde: **Hoard:** a stored away supply of one or more items, often with the connotation that something is being kept from others; **horde:** a large group or crowd, usually living things (people, animals)—often has a negative implication

hurdle/hurtle: **Hurdle:** to leap over; **hurtle:** to move at great speed; often implies great force

hyper-/hypo-: **Hyper-:** a prefix meaning excessive *(hyperactive, hyperemotional)*; **hypo-:** a prefix meaning beneath, lower, or deficient *(hypodermic—under the skin, hypoglycemia—deficient in glucose)*

I

I Could Care Less: incorrect form of "I couldn't care less."

idle/idol/idyll: **Idle:** inactive, not working; **idol:** item of worship; **idyll:** a short poem/prose describing a picturesque, happy scene/event

imaginary/imaginative: **Imaginary:** not real; **imaginative:** being able to imagine

immature/premature: **Immature:** not yet fully grown mentally and/or physically; **premature:** too early

immunity/impunity/impugn: **Immunity:** overall protection—from disease, punishment, liability, etc.; **impunity:** protection from the consequences of an action; **impugn:** to call into question or challenge an idea, statement, etc.

immure/inure: **Immure:** to shut away, usually literally (but also figuratively) within walls; **inure:** to get used to a difficult situation

imply/infer: A distinction that is slowly being lost; **imply** is to hint at something without saying it; **infer** is to draw a conclusion from real or perceived implications

inability/disability: **Inability:** not able; **disability:** usually refers to a permanent or semi-permanent flaw

incite/insight: **Incite:** to prompt into action; **insight:** deep understanding

incredible/incredulous: **Incredible:** difficult or impossible to believe; **incredulous:** dubious, skeptical

inflict/afflict: One **inflicts** something on another, who is then **afflicted**

ingenious/ingenuous/disingenuous: The first two are confused because of spelling; **ingenious:** clever and imaginative; **ingenuous:** innocent, naive; **disingenuous:** less than open or fully honest

innocent/innocuous: **Innocent:** blameless or ingenious; **innocuous:** harmless or inoffensive

intelligent/intellectual: An **intelligent** person has the ability to learn; an **intellectual** uses what he or she has learned and seeks to know more

it's/its: Use the apostrophe *only* in a contraction for **it is** (or it has); otherwise use **its**

J

judicial/judicious: **Judicial** refers only to courts and/or legal proceedings; use **judicious** when describing one who is wise, sound of judgment, etc.

K

karat/carat/caret: A **karat** measures the purity/fineness of gold; a **carat** measures the weight of gems/precious stones; a **caret** is a printer's mark (a sort of upside-down "v") to show places to insert text

knew/new: **Knew:** the past tense of know; **new:** not old

kudos/kudo: **Kudos** means praise and is singular; **kudo** is never correct

L

lama/llama: Lama: a priest; **llama:** a sheep-like animal

latest/last: Although often used interchangeably, **latest** means "most recent," while **last** is final

laudable/laudatory: Laudable: deserving of praise; **laudatory:** expressing praise

lay/lie: Lay is to put in place; **lie** is to take a reclining or prone position

lead/led/lead: Lead, (pronounced lēd), takes as its past tense **led; lead** (pronounced lĕd) refers to the metal

liable/libel/slander: Liable: either responsible for, or open to; **libel:** a *written* untruth; **slander:** a *spoken* untruth

lightening/lightning: Lightening: becoming brighter or less heavy; **lightning:** a weather phenomenon

literally/figuratively/virtually: Literally is used for stating an exact fact; **figuratively** is used for hyperbole; **virtually** is used when something is almost literal or complete, but just falls short

loath/loathe (loathsome): Loath: reluctant, unwilling; **loathe:** to hate, usually violently; note that something *loathed* is *__loathsome__*—the "e" is dropped

lose/loose: **Lose:** misplace; **loose:** not tight

luxuriant/luxurious: **Luxuriant:** growing in abundance; **luxurious:** pertaining to great wealth and/or comfort

M

madding/maddening: **Madding:** crazed, *acting* as if insane; **maddening:** *making* crazy

mantel/mantle: **Mantel:** the framework around a fireplace; although often used only to refer to the shelf on top; **mantle:** a cloak

marital/martial: **Marital:** things dealing with marriage; **martial:** things dealing with war

masterful/masterly: **Masterful:** domineering, over-powering; **masterly:** with great skill, ability

materiel/material: **Materiel:** the equipment and supplies of an organization (often military); **material:** the ingredients of which something is made

may/might: Often used interchangeably; **might** is actually the past of **may**

media/medium: **Media:** the plural of **medium,** but only when referring to communications

mediate/meditate: **Mediate:** to resolve a dispute or argument; **meditate:** to think about

metal/mettle/medal: **Metal:** chemical substance; **mettle;** courage (i.e., a person's substance) **medal:** award for achievement

metaphor/simile: Both compare one thing with another for "poetic" or hyperbolic effect: a **metaphor** states the one thing is the other (*"The moon was a ghostly galleon...."*); a **simile** makes the comparison using "like" or "as" (*"He was as nervous as a long-tailed cat in a room full of rocking chairs."*)

minimal/minimum: These are both "absolutes" and mean the smallest or least; neither should be used to mean simply smaller/lesser

mitigate/militate: **Mitigate:** ease up, make less severe; **militate:** having power, strength, force against something

moot/mute: **Moot:** arguable; its colloquial use has given it the extended meaning of "hypothetical," and therefore not necessary to solving a problem; **mute:** silent

moral/morale: **Moral:** That which is right, correct, altruistic, etc.; **morale:** a state of mind

mull/mule: **Mull:** to think over; **mule:** a beast of burden

N

naval/navel: **naval:** referring to the Navy, or ships in general; **navel:** the belly-button

negligent/negligible: We are **negligent** if we fail to do something we should have done; if it is not worth doing, or of no consequence, it is **negligible**

noisome/noisy: **Noisome:** foul-smelling or disgusting; **noisy:** to make lots of noise

O

obsolete/obsolescent: Similar, but **obsolescent** refers to something that is *becoming* obsolete, but may still be in use; something **obsolete** is no longer in use; for example, a three-year old computer may-be **obsolescent**, but a manual typewriter is **obsolete**

of/have: It is never correct to use **of** in place of **have,** as in *"You should have..."; the contracted form is "'ve" as in "I could've"*

official/officious: **Official:** Anything that comes from a recognized authority (office); **officious:** offensively aggressive

oral/verbal: (Often incorrectly interchanged) **oral:** something spoken aloud; **verbal:** anything written or spoken

ordinance/ordnance: **Ordinance:** a law, regulation; **ordnance:** military weaponry

oversight/omission: An **oversight** is something we miss/leave out inadvertently; an **omission** is deliberate

P

palate/palette/pallet: **Palate:** the roof of the mouth; **palette:** a board used by a painter to mix colors; **pallet:** a type of bed or the platform on which large/heavy items are laid

paradox/paradigm: **Paradox:** apparently mutually exclusive or self-contradictory terms stated together for dramatic effect: "less is more" (paradoxes of two words are called *oxymorons*: "jumbo shrimp"); **paradigm**: a pattern or example

pedal/peddle: **Pedal:** Operate with one's feet, like a bicycle; **peddle:** sell

perquisite/prerequisite: **Perquisite:** something "extra" added as compensation, a "perk"; **prerequisite:** something needed before some action can be achieved

persecute/prosecute: **Persecute:** harass, torment; **prosecute:** to pursue legal action

pore/pour: **pore:** a small, natural opening in the skin; **pour:** the flow of liquid (**pore** can also mean "to examine," as in "to pore over")

practical/practicable: Anything that can be done is **practicable;** if it can be done sensibly it is **practical**

precede/proceed: **Precede:** to come before; **proceed:** to go before

precedence/precedent: **Precedence:** to have priority over something else; **precedent:** drawn from a similar idea—a law, deed, etc. that has occurred previously that establishes the course of action in a similar situation

premise/premises: **Premise:** an idea on which an argument is based; **premises:** a building and the land it occupies

prescribe/proscribe: **Prescribe:** dictate, order, etc.; **proscribe:** ban

principle/principal: **Principle:** a rule; **principal:** the primary thing/person

puppet/marionette: Although some use the terms interchangeably, properly speaking, only a **marionette** has strings—all others are **puppets**

purposely/purposefully: **Purposely:** deliberately; **purposefully:** determinedly

Q

quiet/quite: **Quiet:** not noisy; **quite:** very

quote/quotation: Use **quote** as a verb, **quotation** as a noun; *"Feel free to **quote** me about the **quotation** from Hemingway"*

R

raise/rise: When an object is **raised**, it **rises**

rational/rationale: **Rational:** reasonable, thoughtful; **rationale:** the reason for doing something, often an excuse for bad behavior

ravage/ravish/ravishing: **Ravage:** destroy, devastate; **ravish:** rape, kidnap for purposes of rape; **ravishing:** most often used for extremely attractive *(**ravishing** beauty)*

ravel/unravel: For reasons best known to our early wordsmiths, **ravel** can mean either tangle or *un*tangle; **unravel** always means untangle

rebellion/revolution: A **rebellion** is an armed resistance to one's government; a **revolution** is the overthrow of that government

recreation/re-creation: **Recreation:** a leisure activity or pastime; **re-creation:** to create anew something from the past

reek/wreak: **Reek:** to stink or give off an offensive odor; **wreak:** to bring about, cause or inflict

regardless/irregardless: **Regardless:** without consideration for consequences, feelings, etc.; **irregardless:** has fallen into common usage, but *regardless* is preferred

regretful/regrettable: One who is filled with sorrow is **regretful;** the *situation* that may have *caused* that sorrow is **regrettable**

rein/reign/rain: Coming from the same root, **rein** and **reign** are often wrongfully interchanged; **rein:** a literal and figurative strap to hold a person/animal under control; **reign:** to rule; **rain** refers to the weather phenomenon

relevant/irrelevant: **Relevant** and its converse, **irrelevant,** mean pertaining to (or *not* pertaining to) the matter at hand; (**revelant** and **irrevelant** *do not exist*)

reluctant/reticent: **Reluctant:** unwilling; **reticent:** silent, shy

remediable/remedial: Something **remediable** can be cured/fixed; something **remedial** is intended to produce the cure/fix

respectful/respective: **Respectful:** showing respect or deference; **respective:** particular, separate, or distinct

retch/wretch: **Retch:** to throw up/vomit; **wretch:** an unfortunate person

S

script/scrip: A **script** (shortening of *manuscript*) is the written text of a play or film; **scrip** is paper given out in place of money during a crisis when actual cash may not be available

seasonal/seasonable: A subtle difference: **seasonal** things are *controlled* by the season, such as seasonal lay-offs in industries that only thrive at specific times of year; **seasonable** things are what is expected or appropriate to the season; warm winters or cold summers would be *unseasonable*

sensuous/sensual: **Sensuous** things are, in essence, *mentally* stimulating (the sensuous pleasures of music); **sensual** things are *physically* stimulating

set/sit: Set means "to place;" **sit** means "be seated"

sight/cite/site: **Sight:** anything having to do with seeing; **cite:** to refer to, usually, but not exclusively, in a written document; **site:** a location

smell/scent/odor: Although sometimes used interchangeably, in proper usage, **smell** is a verb— we smell a scent or odor; further, a **scent** implies something pleasant, an **odor,** less so

stalactite/stalagmite: These are the rock formations in caves that resemble icicles "growing" either down or up from the cave ceiling and floor; (**stalactite:** hangs down; **stalagmite:** goes up)

stationary/stationery: Stationary: unmoving; **stationery:** writing paper

statue/statute: Statue: a three-dimensional likeness; **statute:** a law

straight/strait: Straight: extending in a direction without bending or curving; **strait:** a narrow passage between two things

suit/suite: Although meaning similar things, **suit** (pronounced soot) should be used for cards, clothes and, with a different meaning, court cases; **suite** (pronounced sweet) should be used for music, furniture and rooms

T

tasteful/tasty: Tasteful means to have good taste (in clothes, books, music, etc.); **tasty** means to taste good

than/then: Than is used as a comparative; **then** for subsequence (*"If you are older **than** he is, **then**, it must follow he is younger **than** you."*)

their/there/they're: Their: belonging to them; **there:** not here; **they're:** contraction for *they are*

to/too/two: **To** indicates movement, *"going to the movies"*; **too:** overly, also; **two:** the number

tortuous/torturous: **Tortuous:** twisting, winding, often with a negative connotation; **torturous:** causing extreme pain

toward/towards: **Towards** is improper; use **toward**

tract/track: **Tract:** an area of land; also a short treatise or pamphlet on a religious, political, or similar subject; **track:** a path

troupe/troop: Both mean a group of people working together, but **troupe** should be reserved for entertainers (actors, dancers, etc.); a **trooper** is a soldier or police officer, but one who perseveres through hardship is a **trouper**

trusty/trustee: A **trusty** is a convict given special privileges, usually for good behavior; a **trustee** is someone legally entrusted with administering or decision making for others

turbid/turgid: **Turbid:** cloudy, confused; **turgid:** swollen, overblown

U

use/utilize: These two words mean the same thing; use **use;** it is more concise

use to/suppose to: Incorrect form of **used to** and **supposed to**.

V

valued/valuable: Valued: highly thought of, esteemed; **valuable:** worth a lot

venial/venal: Venial: a minor transgression easily forgiven; **venal:** corrupt

verbal/oral: (Often incorrectly interchanged) **verbal:** anything written or spoken; **oral:** something spoken aloud

vice/vise: Vice: a bad habit; **vise:** a tool for clamping something in place

W

waist/waste: Waist: the middle part of the body, just above the navel; **waste:** refuse, trash

wave/waive: Wave: moving an object up and down or back and forth; **waive:** to relinquish

wax/wane: Wax: grow in strength/intensity; **wane:** shrink in strength/intensity, usually slowly

way/weigh: **Way:** direction; **weigh:** to raise up (things used to be "weighed" by raising and lowering them); the phrase in the Navy hymn, "Anchors *a-weigh,*" means "raise the anchors"; also refers to the mass of an object

wear/where: **Wear:** to have clothing; **where:** interrogative for what place or location

weather/whether: **Weather:** climatic conditions; **whether** indicates a choice

which/witch: **Which** means either/or; **witch** is the woman on a broomstick

whose/who's: **Whose:** The possessive form of "who"; **who's:** may appear to be the possessive, but is actually the contraction "who is" or "who has"

Y

yolk/yoke: **Yolk:** the yellow part of an egg; **yoke:** the crossbar that holds oxen in place, also used for domination ("under the **yoke** of the oppressor"), both literally and figuratively

your/you're: **Your:** the possessive of *you;* **you're:** the contraction for *you are*

Z

ZIP code/zip code: **ZIP** is an acronym for **Z**one **I**mprovement **P**rogram and should always be capitalized, as should all acronyms